An Agile A(Transformation Survival Guide: Working with Organizational Culture

Michael Sahota

Forewords by Jurgen Appelo and Henrik Kniberg

Foreword by Jurgen Appelo

All models are useful, but some fail faster than others. That's my own adaptation of George Box' much more famous quote, "All models are wrong, but some are useful."

In this small but valuable book, Michael Sahota gives the reader many useful models for working with Agile organizations, and organizations that try to become Agile. Michael's book taught me that this often requires a transformation, which is much harder than a simple adoption. Learning how to make a decent coffee is an adoption. Becoming a barista is a transformation. An adoption changes only what you do. A transformation changes what you are.

Of course, this distinction is just another model, but a very useful one. When we want to change the world of software development, we must learn how to transform organizational cultures. It's not enough to simply adopt some practices. I hear it almost every day. In my courses, at conferences, and when I enjoy a "roving coffee" with Agile practitioners in cities that I visit across the world. People don't struggle so much with the adoption of Agile practices. They struggle with the transformation to the Agile mindset, because many organizational cultures actively resist it.

From the best change management literature I learned that changing organizational culture cannot be done with a simple 5-step plan. It is a lot of work actually. It requires understanding the current culture, applying different models, adapting new ideas to fit in traditional contexts, shortening feedback cycles, addressing both the people and their environment, alternating between continuous change and radical change, and experimenting in safe-to-fail ways. And lots of coffee.

Fortunately, Michael wrote this book to make life a bit easier for us. The different models he describes may not always be right. But from complexity thinking we can learn that you only get a good understanding of a complex problem by using multiple incomplete perspectives. Many weak models together can significantly boost our sense-making.

Michael's story in this book is small, but it makes a lot of sense. I have already adopted some of his ideas in my classes. I might even say, it has transformed a bit of my thinking.

- Jurgen Appelo

Foreword by Henrik Kniberg

When I attended my first Agile conference I was dazzled by the presence of the Gurus - the people who defined Agile and wrote the books. But, listening to what they were actually saying, I realized to my dismay that they were saying different things, and even disagreeing with each other sometimes. The big learning point for me was "Darn, I have to actually Think For Myself!". Listen to the gurus, read the books, but then think for yourself.

However, Thinking For Yourself doesn't mean ignoring years of accumulated wisdom. It means building up a personal toolkit - a repertoire of models and thinking tools to help you make sense of the world around you. Without such a toolkit you are at the mercy of Gut Feel, which is a great tool but can only take you so far.

Michael has done us a great favor - he has taken the essence of a number of models and books on organizational change, and condensed them to a down-to-earth illustrated overview that is immediately applicable for any coach, manager, or other change agent. This book has an unusually high signal-to-noise ratio. It is straight to the point and, instead of delving into the gory details of each model, Michael provides a high level description - what the model is about and when to apply it - and a reference for where to read more.

The book is refreshing because Michael doesn't hold back - he challenges many wide-held assumptions among us Agile Coaches, and essentially tells us "Here's why you and I suck, and how we can suck less!". Sometimes a friendly slap in the face is what we need to stay alert!

And, to keep everything anchored in reality, he provides plenty of concrete examples and case studies - even a handy checklist! A nice balance between theory (understanding Why), and practice (understanding How).

One thing I've learned as coach and change agent, is that things never turn out as expected (and when they do, that itself is unexpected...). Sometimes a long, on-site coaching engagement ends up with everything reverting back to The Old Way within a year. Conversely, sometimes a short inspirational seminar becomes the seed that ultimately changes the whole organization. Sometimes having lunch with the right person at the right time has bigger impact than years of focused coaching and facilitation.

Michael's book provides a way to make sense of the randomness.

Because it isn't random, it is just complex.

Thank you Michael for unrandomizing the world a bit for us!

- Henrik Kniberg

Acknowledgements

"If I have seen further, it is by standing on the shoulders of giants." – Isaac Newton

I would like to thank Henrik Kniberg who has contributed so much open source material to the Agile community and inspired me to write a free eBook to pay it forward. I also appreciate him taking the time to write one of the forewords.

I would like to thank the attendees of workshops with early incarnations of this material – XPToronto, SoCal Lean Kanban, Agile Tour Toronto, and Agile New England. Your comments, challenges and reflections have helped in immeasurable ways.

Thanks to all the people who read my blog posts throughout 2011 on this topic and provided valuable feedback.

A big thanks to Michael Spayd for first introducing me to the Schneider culture model and for conducting a survey of Agilistas.

For sure this work would not exist but for Mike Cottemeyer's differentiation of adoption and transformation.

Thank you to the review team for feedback: Chris Williams, Irene Kuhn, Armond Mehrabian, Krishan Mathis, Bernie Jansen, Ed Willis, Eric Willeke, Karl Scotland, Sabine Canditt, Todd Charron, Bob Sarni. Olaf Lewitz in particular deserves distinction by providing an extraordinary quantity of valuable comments, questions and challenges.

I would like to thank those who directly contributed to this work as well as reviewing: Olivier Gourment for contributing a case study; Jeff Anderson, Olaf Lewitz, Jon Stahl, and Karl Scotland and Alexei Zheglov for sharing their challenges and alternate visions in the appendix.

I would also like to thank Alistair McKinnell, Jason Little, Declan Whelan for providing feedback on the Methods & Tools article that formed a chapter in this book and to John McFadyen and Dave Snowden for feedback on the Cynefin section.

I am very appreciative of Jurgen Appelo for taking time out of his busy schedule to write a foreword.

And of course a big shout out for my daughter Scarlett who provided original art with the jigsaw puzzle and butterfly transformation drawings.

Wow! Even a small book such as this benefits from so much help

 - Michael Sahota

Table of Contents

Foreword by Jurgen Appelo iii

Foreword by Henrik Kniberg v

Acknowledgements vii

Table of Contents ix

Introduction.. xi

Part 1: Agile in Crisis 1
Agile Failure is Pervasive 1
Agile is Due for Failure.. 3
Culture is the #1 Challenge with Agile Adoption 4

Part 2: Agile Culture 6
Agile is not a Process – it Defines a Culture 6
Understanding Culture through the Schneider Model................... 7
Agile Culture is about Collaboration and Cultivation.................... 9
The Agile Manifesto and Principles Define Agile Culture............ 10
Analysis Approach (For the Curious)................................... 11
Culture Model Lets Us Ask Useful Questions............................. 12
Kanban Culture is Aligned with Control.................................. 12
Wait a Minute - Kanban is Agile, isn't it? 14
Kanban is a Good Tool 14
Kanban as a Trojan Horse or Gateway Drug................................. 15
Kanban+Agile = Agile... 15
Software Craftsmanship is about Competence 16
Why We Need to Care 17
Working with Your Culture.. 18
Understanding Culture.. 19
Working with Other Cultures 20
Culture Adapters... 20
How to Change Culture is Another Story................................... 24
Summary... 24

Part 3: Adoption and Transformation Survival Guide............**25**
  Defining Adoption and Transformation......................................**25**
  A Framework for Understanding Adoption
    and Transformation **25**
  Adoption of Agile Practices in Mismatched Culture..............**27**
    Avoid Agile Manifesto and Scrum...28
    Agile Adoption Patterns..29
    Becoming Agile in an Imperfect World...30
    Case Study: Large Financial...30
  Adoption and Transformation in a Supportive Culture..............**31**
    Lead with Agile Manifesto and Scrum..32
    Fearless Change...33
    Inspect and Adapt with Enterprise Transition Team.....................34
    ADAPT 35
    Containers, Differences and Exchanges...36
    Cynefin Framework...37
    Case Study of Agile Adoption in a Supportive Culture 39
  Agile Transformation **40**
    Is Agile Transformation Possible? 41
    Accidental Agile Transformation is Damaging Companies...........43
    Kotter Model for Organizational Change.......................................45
    Transformational Leadership 47
  Other Approaches to Organizational Change.............................**49**

Where to go next? **51**
  Checklist for Change Agents **51**

References..**53**

About the Author **61**

Alternate Views and Opinions **63**
  Culture as Context for Agile Adoption and Transformation.........63
  You Kanban is not my Kanban 64
  Kanban is more than just Control Culture.....................................65
  Kanban is about Transformation, too!...66
  Scrum vs. Kanban 67

Introduction

The Agile community suffers a significant confusion between adoption and transformation. Sadly, change agents talk of adopting Agile and not about transforming the culture of a company to support the Agile mindset. The sad consequence of this myopia is of change agents accidentally undertaking a transformation without full buy-in or understanding of the organizational consequences. The typical result is failure.

There are few models in our community that guide Agile change agents in understanding when to use adoption and when to use transformation. For sure, there is a substantial body of knowledge on specific adoption and transformation techniques, but little to inform a change agent what moves to make and why to make them.

This survival guide provides a simple framework that can be used to understand and plan Agile change work. The framework can also be helpful if you are working with Kanban or Software Craftsmanship. I have found it immensely useful, as have session participants who have learned it. This framework helped me move out of "unconscious incompetence" as a change agent and become conscious of the choices I am making. This awareness has allowed me to start the climb toward competence.

The first step in mitigating a problem is to acknowledge that you have one. The problem at hand is the high levels of failure with companies adopting or transforming to Agile. Some of the root causes are discussed in the first part of this book to motivate the need for a survival guide.

If you do not manage culture, it manages you. Much of Agile adoption failures are a result of not understanding organizational culture. The second part of this book explains how to use organizational culture to understand Agile, Kanban and Software Craftsmanship movements. It also covers how to use the Schneider culture model to assess your organization's culture and some ways to work effectively with it.

The third part of this book proposes a framework for understanding and selecting adoption and transformation approaches appropriate to a variety of contexts. An overview of key adoption and transformation methods is presented. The framework provides the basic knowledge needed to approach Agile change in organizations.

Part 1: Agile in Crisis

Agile Failure is Pervasive

Agile adoption and transformation efforts are experiencing high failure rates in many industries and organizations. 84% of respondents in the Agile Development Survey reported that they had experienced a failed Agile project [VersionOne]. Only 16% of respondents had not experienced failure.

I have conducted my own informal research on this topic. I asked people to rate on a scale of 0 to 5 how much success they have had with Agile where 0 indicated no success and 5 indicated all projects were successful. The average out of about 130 respondents at four different sessions was 2.7. Not very good. See the informal Failure Survey results below in graphic and table formats. Please note that people self-rated based on their own definitions for "success" and "failure".

Where	When	0	1	2	3	4	5	Count	Average
Play4Agile	Feb-2010		1	6	5	1		13	2.5
XP Toronto	May-2011	1	3	7	10	5		26	2.6
Agile Tour Toronto	Nov-2011		5	12	23	4		44	2.6
Agile New England	Dec-2011		1	8	30	10		49	3.0

One may observe that there is strong consistency in the average results with only minor variation. I do not think that any clear conclusions can be drawn regarding the variance or trends.

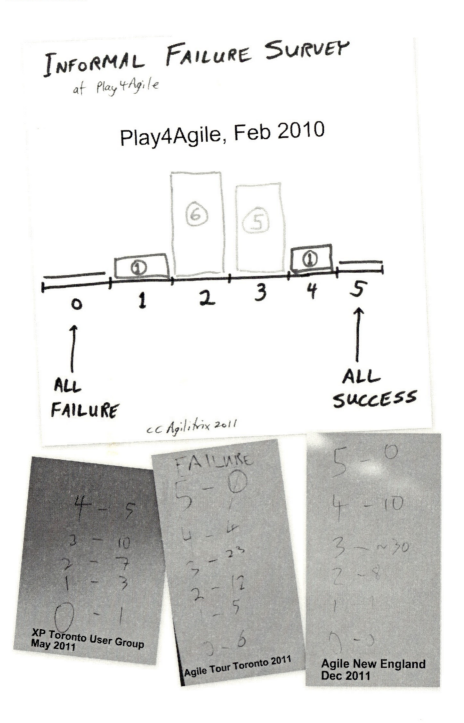

2

Agile is Due for Failure

Let us consider some common reasons for failure and why - as a relatively new concept - Agile seems due for problems.

Let us consider where Agile is on Michael Moore's Crossing the Chasm technology adoption curve. The diagram below shows Agile crossing the chasm. In the early stages, visionaries provide strong management support and have a high tolerance for change.

One key requirement for success with the early majority is a "whole product" consisting of the core idea surrounded by everything needed to make it successful as illustrated below. Some elements of the whole product are present, while others are lacking or even undefined. The continued absence of the whole product is one indicator that Agile is not sufficiently mature for mainstream. But there is an even greater problem: thinking of *Agile as a product* is a *poisoned metaphor* as it does not reflect Agile as a cultural system or mindset.

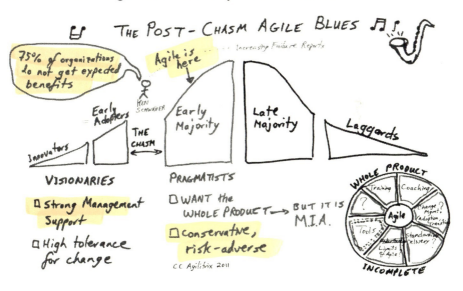

Martin Fowler defines Semantic Diffusion as the process whereby you have a word (e.g. Agile) that is coined by a person or group but then gets spread through the wider community in a way that weakens that definition [Fowler]. This weakening risks losing the definition entirely - and with it any usefulness to the term. I certainly have met people who claim to be Agile and understand the practices but do not understand the Agile mindset. It is increasingly common to find Agile "practitioners" who understand the practices, but do not understand the values and principles. The argument here is that Agile is bound to fail as its message and meaning become garbled.

As word gets out about Agile, it follows a common pattern observed with many technological adoptions where there is hype and disillusionment as illustrated in the diagram below [Wikimedia – "Hype Cycle"]. Agile has passed the *peak of inflated expectations* and is heading for the *trough of disillusionment* [Stack Overflow – "Is Agile Development is Dead?"]. One might consider this book as a step towards accelerating this process by calling out failure and providing early steps up the *slope of enlightenment*.

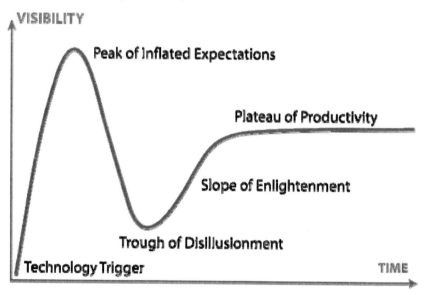

Culture is the #1 Challenge with Agile Adoption

The results of the State of Agile Development Survey are astonishing in terms of the severity and breadth of challenges organizations face with Agile adoption [VersionOne]. The #1 barrier to further Agile adoption at companies is *cultural change* (see diagram below), a problem reported by 52% of the respondents. Even this number may be understated because cultural impacts are challenging to identify.

So, how important is company culture? Edgar Schein, a professor at MIT Sloan School of Management, says "If you do not manage culture, it manages you, and you may not even be aware of the extent to which this is happening."

BARRIERS TO FURTHER AGILE ADOPTION

For over half of respondents, the inability to change their organization's culture was the biggest problem. Budget constraints had the lowest impact on further adoption (14%).

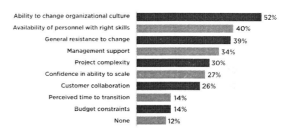

Barrier	Percentage
Ability to change organizational culture	52%
Availability of personnel with right skills	40%
General resistance to change	39%
Management support	34%
Project complexity	30%
Confidence in ability to scale	27%
Customer collaboration	26%
Perceived time to transition	14%
Budget constraints	14%
None	12%

Part 2: Agile Culture

Agile is not a Process – it Defines a Culture

But what does this have to do with Agile?

Well, what is Agile? The consensus definition is provided by the decade old Agile Manifesto [Agile Manifesto]. Agile is an *idea* supported by a set of *values* and *beliefs*. In other words Agile defines a *target culture* for successful delivery of software. This book will explore more on Agile's cultural model later.

Agile is commonly described as a process or a family of processes. This is true, but a dangerous and incorrect abstraction. Sadly, I have communicated this misleading message out of ignorance many times. If Agile were just a process family, then we wouldn't be seeing culture as a prevalent problem.

All too commonly, Agile is bought and sold as a *product*. Companies have problems such as too slow time to market or poor quality and want a solution. Agile benefits are touted and a project is kicked off with Agile as the solution. Dave Thomas coined the concept of the *Agile Tooth Fairy* where Agile coaches can swoop in and sprinkle magic dust on troubled projects to correct years of atrophy and neglect [Thomas]. This is a myth: Agile is not a silver bullet.

Agile is about a fundamental shift in thinking. Tobias Mayer has written that Scrum is much more about changing the way we think than it is a process [Mayer]. Bob Hartman has a great presentation on this topic – Doing Agile isn't the same as being Agile [Hartmann]. The essential point is that we are "Doing Agile" when we follow practices and we are "Being Agile" when we act with an Agile mindset. Experienced practitioners know the practices are a means to an end.

Mike Cottmeyer wrote a series of great posts on how companies are adopting Agile, not transforming to Agile [Cottemeyer] He has greatly helped the community disambiguate *adoption* from *transformation* as

6

these terms were, and still are, used interchangeably. Mike makes this distinction:

- Adoption is about changing the 'agile doing' side of the equation

- Transformation is about changing the 'agile being' side of the equation

Independently, Israel Gat was speaking about the relationship between Agile and culture in How we do things around here in order to succeed [Gat]. His observation was that Agile adoption will trigger conflict due to cultural mismatches between groups within a company. He suggests that we need to be aware of these so that we can mitigate them. Pete Behrens has documented case studies in using Culture as a way to support Agility [Behrens]

To be successful, we need to start thinking about *Agile as a culture and not as a product or family of processes.*

In the next section I will introduce a model for culture that can be used to understand culture at your organization. The following sections explain the unique cultures of Agile, Kanban, and Software Craftsmanship. In the last section, I provide a guide to assess how well a particular approach fits with your organization's culture.

Understanding Culture through the Schneider Model

We need to define what we mean by culture before exploring Agile further. In this section, I will introduce the *Schneider Culture Model* based on William Schneider's book [Schneider - The Reengineering Alternative: A plan for making your current culture work]. Although there are many different ways of thinking about corporate culture, this model has been selected since it leads to actionable plans.

What is a culture model? A culture model tells us about the values and norms within a group or company. It identifies what is important as well as how people approach work and each other. For example, one culture may value stability and order. In this case clearly defined processes are valued and there is a strong expectation of conformance to process rather than innovation and creativity.

The Schneider Culture Model defines four distinct cultures:

1. *Collaboration* culture is about working together
2. *Control* culture is about getting and keeping control
3. *Competence* culture is about being the best
4. *Cultivation* culture is about learning and growing with a sense of purpose

The diagram below summarizes the Schneider Culture Model. Each of the four cultures are depicted – one in each quadrant. Each has a name, a "descriptive quote", a picture, and some words that characterize that quadrant. Please take a moment to read through the diagram and get a sense of the model and where your company fits.

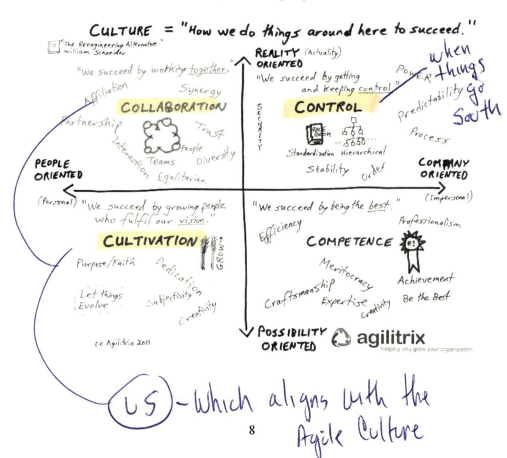

US – Which aligns with the Agile Culture

Another aspect of the Schneider model is the axes that indicate the focus of an organization:

1. Horizontal axis : People Oriented (Personal) vs. Company Oriented (Impersonal)
2. Vertical axis: Reality Oriented (Actuality) vs. Possibility Oriented

This provides a way to see relationships between the cultures. For example, Control culture is more compatible with Collaboration or Competence cultures than with Cultivation culture. In the Schneider model, Cultivation culture is the opposite of Control culture; learning and growing is opposite of security and structure. Similarly, Collaboration is the opposite of Competence.

"All models are wrong, some are useful" – George Box, statistician. All models are an approximation of reality and it is important to remember that we are ignoring minor discrepancies so that we can perform analysis and have meaningful discourse. Also, we may wish to consider other models such as Spiral Dynamics to understand cultural evolution [Beck, Cowan].

In the Schneider model, no one culture type is considered better than another. Please refer to the book for details the strengths and weaknesses of each. Depending on the type of work, one type of culture may be a better fit.

Schneider suggests that most companies have a single dominant culture with elements from the other three culture quadrants. Other cultural elements are encouraged as long as they serve the dominant culture. Different departments or groups (e.g. development vs. operations) typically have different sub-cultures. These differences can lead to conflict.

Agile Culture is about Collaboration and Cultivation

Michael Spayd has done the community a great service by undertaking a culture survey of Agilistas Culture Survey of Agile [Spayd]. See diagram below for results. His landmark results show that *Agile practitioners* have a particular culture profile and identified the key elements as *Collaboration* and *Cultivation*. The results suggest that Agile is all about the *people*. Interestingly, the survey included Scrum, XP, as well as Kanban software practitioners.

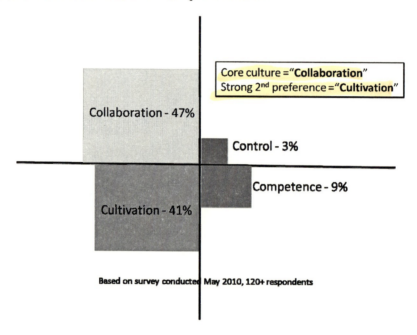

The Agile Manifesto and Principles Define Agile Culture

The Agile Manifesto and twelve principles – even after ten years – are still the reference for what is considered Agile. Consider the following diagram, where the values and principles are mapped to the Schneider model.

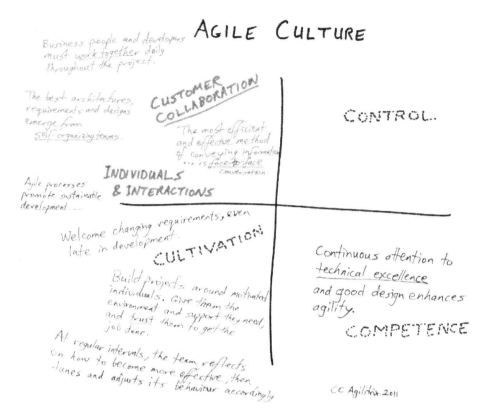

It can be seen that there is high density of values and practices that are aligned with *Collaboration* and *Cultivation*. Note that there were no elements related to Control culture and only one related to Competence culture. This is strikingly similar to the result obtained by Michael Spayd in his survey of Agilistas.

Analysis Approach (For the Curious)

Some of you may be curious as to how I arrived at this result and the ones that follow.

For each value or principle, I analyzed how well it was aligned with each of the cultures. If there was a strong affinity, I associated it with that culture. For example, Customer Collaboration was very easy since it identifies success through people working together. Some items seemed to be orthogonal to the Schneider culture model. For example, working software, didn't really seem to suggest one culture over another. Well, it may weakly suggest Competence culture, but only a bit. As a result, it is not depicted in the diagram above. Other items were a best guess based on my current understanding.

Alexei Zhegloz suggested to me that this approach is like throwing darts on a dartboard. Each value or principle is an individual dart. The dartboard is the Schneider model. Some darts will land on board in a particular part of a culture quadrant while others will miss entirely. After throwing ten or so "darts", we can see how they scatter, but we don't need to care too much whether any individual dart throw was accurate. This analysis method is used to illustrate the cultural bias of a system of thought.

These results have been validated through group workshops where participants performed the same activity after having an explanation of the culture model. [Sahota "Culture Workshop"]

Culture Model Lets Us Ask Useful Questions

Agile is about people. Not such a startling conclusion: seems we all know that.

What is interesting is that when we start thinking about Agile as a *specific culture* we can now use this for asking interesting questions:

- What is the culture in my company now?
- How well is the culture aligned with Agile?
- What problems can I expect due to misalignment?

More on this in the section *Working with your Culture* below.

Kanban Culture is Aligned with Control   *– used to visually manage work*

I am choosing an insightful post by David Anderson as the basis for my analysis [Anderson – "Principles of the Kanban Method"]. David is arguably the main leader of the Kanban/Software school with his book, a very active mailing list, and the Lean Software and Systems

Consortium. I choose this post as it is a concise summary of the principles outlined in his book, Kanban [Anderson – "Kanban"].

As with the Agile manifesto, I have taken the Kanban principles and aligned them with the Schneider culture model. As can be seen in the following diagram, Kanban is largely aligned with Control culture with Competence as a secondary influence.

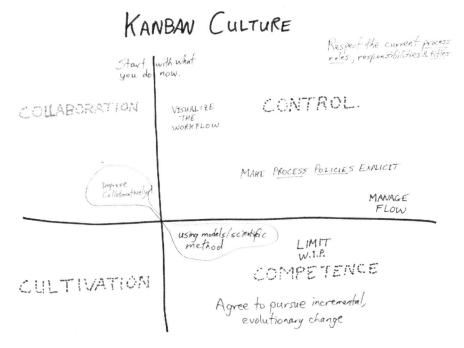

Control cultures live and breathe policies and process. Kanban has this in spades. Control culture is also about creating a clear and orderly structure for managing the company - exactly what Kanban does well. Control cultures focus on the company/system (not people) and current state (not future state). This is a good description for the starting place used with Kanban.

What is really interesting from a cultural analysis perspective is the principle: Improve collaboratively using models and the scientific method. According to the Schneider model, these two concepts don't mix since they are from opposing cultures. So how can this work? According to Schneider, other cultural elements can be present as long as they support the core culture. So having some people focus is fine as long as it supports controlling the work.

The notion of evolutionary or controlled change can also be compatible with a Control culture if it is used to maintain the existing organizational structure and hierarchy.

Karl Scotland has an alternate set of principles that define Kanban [Scotland – "Thoughts on Kanban Thinking"]. Interestingly, these principles also fall in the Control and Competence quadrants of the model.

Wait a Minute - Kanban is Agile, isn't it?

Mike Burrows wrote a very influential post where he argues that Kanban satisfies each of the Agile Principles [Burrows]. Now that I am studying this from the perspective of culture, I see that this is only weakly the case.

Agile and Kanban for sure share a common community, and many practices may be cross-adopted. However, they are fundamentally promoting different perspectives. Agile is first about people and Kanban is first about the system. Yes, people are important in Kanban too, but this is secondary to the system.

So is Kanban Agile? I used to think so. I don't any more. I can see now how the belief - that Kanban is Agile - is harmful since the cultural biases are different.

Kanban is a Good Tool

Sometimes when I share this analysis where Kanban is linked to Control culture, I get a strong negative reaction, as Control culture is anathema to knowledge work. To avoid any misunderstanding, I would like to clarify a few things:

1. I love Kanban and think it is great. We need more of it in the world. See my related blog post where I argued that some

situations are a better fit for Kanban vs. Scrum [Sahota – "Scrum or Kanban? Yes!"].

2. I am not saying people who use Kanban are control freaks or prefer command and control. What I am saying is that if your company has a Control culture, then Kanban is a better tool to help vs. Scrum.

Please see the appendix for alternate views of Kanban provided by reviewers.

Kanban as a Trojan Horse or Gateway Drug

The gateway drug theory states that softer drugs (Kanban) can lead to harder drugs (Scrum, XP). This is a great metaphor because this theory has been proven as well as dis-proven. To quote David Anderson "we are only beginning to understand the differences between Scrum and Kanban".

With Kanban, there are documented cases of teams spontaneously collaborating, learning, and noticing/solving problems. This has been my experience as well and would confirm the hypothesis of Kanban as a Trojan horse (containing Agile on the inside).

It is good when people work to improve their environments at a steady pace. Many organizations are not ready for a radical overhaul (even though they may desperately need one). For companies like these, Kanban is a great place to start. Getting off the sofa and going for a marathon (Scrum) may cause a heart attack; for many it may be better to start by jogging around the block (Kanban). We will explore this topic subject further through an exploration of adoption and transformation.

Kanban+Agile = Agile

It is possible to practice an Agile mindset with Kanban as a starting place for evolving the process. In this situation, the focus is around Agile values and principles where policies and processes are used to support people's work. Such an approach may be appropriate where

Scrum or XP are not a good fit for the environment. See CrystalBan as an option for integrating people into Kanban [Scotland – "Crystallising Kanban"].

Olaf Lewitz argues that Kanban can and should be used just as Agile is - to challenge the status quo. It's primary purpose is to provide a sense-respond loop that can be used to drive change in organizations. He argues that "the people are the system" and that any change program must involve them as a central component.

Software Craftsmanship is about Competence

The rise of anemic Scrum has caused dismay in the Agile community. "Uncle Bob" Martin crystallized this problem when he coined the fifth Agile manifesto value of Craftsmanship over Crap (Execution) [Martin – "Quintessence"]. This gave rise to the much needed community of Software Craftsmanship ["Manifesto for Software Craftsmanship"].

I have already established that the Agile community is focused on Collaboration and Cultivation at the expense of Competence. We as a community of software professionals do need to pay attention to Competence and technical excellence for long term sustainability. For further information on this, see Uncle Bob's recent article [Martin – "The Land that Scrum Forgot"].

The diagram below relates parts of the Software Craftsmanship Manifesto to cultures identified in the Schneider model.

CULTURE OF SOFTWARE CRAFTSMANSHIP

COLLABORATION

CONTROL

PRODUCTIVE PARTNERSHIPS

CULTIVATION

CRAFTSMANSHIP* OVER CRAP

COMPETENCE

x 5th Agile Manifesto Value

WELL CRAFTED SOFTWARE

"raising the bar of professional software development"

CC Agilitrix 2011

COMMUNITY OF PROFESSIONALS

Not surprisingly, there is a big focus on Competence Culture. This culture achieves success by being the best. And craftsmanship is about being the best software developers possible.

The value of *productive partnerships* stands alone. The main sentiment is about working together with customers to produce valuable software that solves real problems. Not just code monkeys.

Why We Need to Care

Craftsmanship *needs to exist* to make sure that the technical practices promoted by XP are used to support sustainable development and don't get lost in fluffy-bunny Agile culture. Things like: refactor mercilessly, do the simplest thing that could possibly work, Test Driven Development (TDD), Acceptance Test Driven Development (ATDD), continuous integration, continuous deployment, shared code ownership, clean code, etc.

The creation and existence of a separate movement to support a Competence culture that exists outside of Agile, supports the assessment of Agile culture as focused on Collaboration and Cultivation and not Competence.

As a final footnote before departing the culture of Software Craftsmanship, I would like to reflect that this manifesto does not accurately reflect a key aspect of the movement: a *deep commitment to learning and growth* (Cultivation culture). This is a value that exists to support the goal of excellence in software construction.

Working with Your Culture

Consider the following diagram illustrating how Agile, Kanban, and Craftsmanship principles align with various cultures. The shapes illustrate the dominant culture for each of Agile, Kanban and Software Craftsmanship based on the analysis earlier in earlier sections.

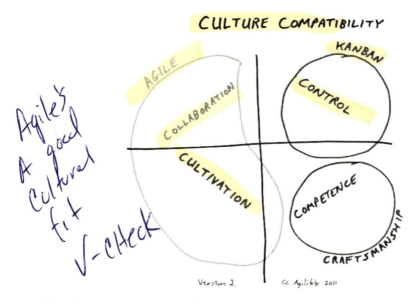

The diagram can be used as a *guide* to determine what approach *builds on the dominant culture* at your company.

- Control Culture –> Lead with Kanban
- Competence Culture –> Lead with Software Craftsmanship
- Collaboration or Cultivation Culture –> Lead with aspects of Agile that align with the organizations culture. e.g. Vision and Retrospectives for Cultivation Culture.

It is not intended that this guide be used without consideration of other aspects of organizational culture and context.

Of course, many readers may be interested in how to change the organizational culture from Control to Collaboration, Cultivation and Competence. This is discussed in detail in the section on transformation.

Understanding Culture

The starting point for working with your culture work is to understand it. Schneider describes a survey you can give to staff [Schneider – "Survey"] and suggests using the survey results as a starting point for culture workshops with a diverse group of staff. In my own personal experience, I find the workshop alone is more accurate (as reported by participants) and results in a deeper understanding and buy-in.

Management guru Peter Drucker says *"Culture ... is singularly persistent* ... In fact, changing behaviour works only if it is based on the existing 'culture'"*. The implication here is that it is not possible to just switch over from a Control culture to an Agile one.

A central premise of Schneider's book is that it is essential to work with the existing culture rather than oppose it. There are several suggestions for using cultural information to guide decision-making:

1. Evaluate key problems in the context of culture. Sometimes changes are needed to bring the culture into alignment with the core culture.
2. Sometimes the culture is too extreme (e.g. too much Cultivation without any controls – or vice versa!), and elements from other cultures are needed to bring it back into balance.

3. Consider the possibility of creating interfaces/adapters/facades to support mismatches between departments or groups.

Working with Other Cultures

Consider the diagram below showing effective ways of working with culture.

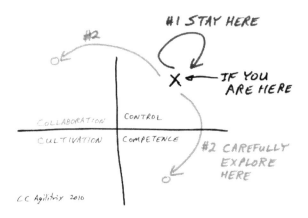

Option #1 illustrates that the easiest option is to work with the existing dominant culture (in this case Control). Option #2 is to carefully explore adjacent cultures in ways that support the core culture of the group. Choice of direction may be guided by what the secondary culture of the organization is. The idea here is to work with the culture, and not to fight against it.

Culture Adapters

A very powerful way to think about introducing a foreign culture such as Agile to an organization is through a cellular model. Consider a successful transformation of one team or group to Agile.

Imagine that the team is very excited about the new way of working. Since this chapter is all about transformation, they exist in the context of some other culture. The team is not that excited about all of the organizational barriers and limits on productivity and success. So, what typically happens is they start to push back on the needs and requirements of other groups that are not adding value to the team and to the customers.

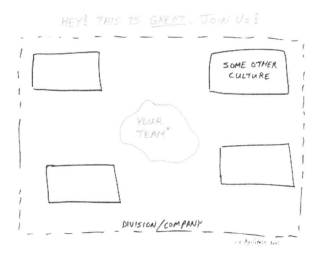

The result sounds like a B-movie: "Attack of the Organizational Antibodies!" In the human body, we have antibodies (Killer T-Cells) that are designed to eliminate foreign elements to keep us healthy. In a similar way, organizations will react to the introduction of a foreign culture system such as Agile. These are the elements that work hard to preserve the status quo.

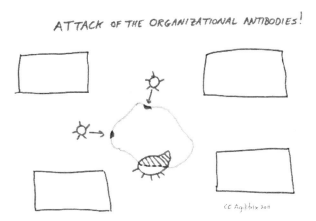

The movie doesn't have to have a bad ending. One common pattern is to build adapters or translators around the foreign culture so that it fits within the overall culture. These are depicted in the diagram below as shapes surrounding and protecting the team. In this situation, the adapter allows the team to blend in with the overall organizational culture and avoid triggering the antibodies.

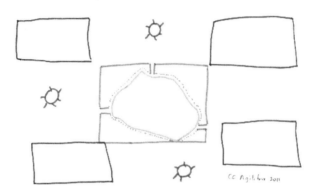

In practical terms, the adapter could take the form of a Microsoft Project Plan that has no value to the customers or team but is required by the organization. Another might be team use of a peer-based review for merit increases that still gets submitted by the manager since the system requires input only from her.

This sounds like a lot of effort! Is it worth it? The value is equal to the benefits derived from Agile less the cost of adapter maintenance. Assuming there is good value in the team's new state of functioning, then sadly some of that productivity will be lost maintaining the adapters. But this is a much better situation to be in compared to getting attacked by organizational antibodies. The adapters are part of the cost of doing business. Like taxes.

Lean differentiates between different types of waste in organizations. Type I Muda (waste) are non value added tasks that are *required* at the current time. Type II Muda are non value added tasks that can be removed immediately. Maintaining the adapters is type I since the environment requires them.

> Case Study: In one organization, I was introducing Scrum and the PMO requested us to produce a project plan. I correctly observed that the plan would not add any value and became engulfed in an ongoing pitched battle with the PMO. Sure, it saved a small amount of work, but in the long run it created enemies of the Agile transition within the company.

> Fortunately, the team was very successful and the manager himself acted as the adapter. He worked hard to protect the team and to satisfy all the external organizational requirements. After two years of struggle, he was still at it and found it wore down on him.

> Case Study by Olivier Gourment: I introduced pair programming in an organization where code reviews were mandatory, but did not want to go as far as doing pair programming. I just presented them as a "better code review". One way to look at it is that the reviewer and developer collaborate earlier on the code to review. From the outside, it just looked like we were only doing code reviews. Pair programming is really something you need to try before you understand its benefits. In that case, it saved a huge amount of time because the web framework was new for the whole team, and standards needed to emerge.

The model above points a way to success with Agile transformation – *it is possible to transform one team or group provided that care and attention is provided to satisfying the requirements of the larger organization.* It would appear that the adapter strategy is not sustainable in the long term. It may, however, be a feasible strategy to consider this a first step before a wider organizational change initiative.

Joseph Pelrine has a thorough discussion of the problem of mismatches between Agile teams and their environments in [Pelrine]. It is also a good explanation of social complexity thinking.

How to Change Culture is Another Story

Changing culture is very difficult. More on this topic will be discussed in the next chapter on Agile Transformation.

Summary

Congratulations! You now have the Schneider Culture Model - an easy-to-use tool for assessing culture in your company. Once you know your company's culture, you will be aware of how it is influencing many aspects of day-to-day work. More importantly, you can use the cultural fit model to decide what approach - Agile, Kanban, or Software Craftsmanship - will best fit with your organization if you want to work with the existing culture. Of course, if your interest is in challenging the status quo to help build great teams and organizations, keep on reading.

Part 3: Adoption and Transformation Survival Guide

Defining Adoption and Transformation

Adoption is a term that applies to a product or process. For example, "we are adopting GoogleDocs to replace Microsoft Office" or "we are adopting a new procurement process".

It is often used incorrectly as "we are adopting Agile". As we have established that Agile is a mindset and a culture, it cannot be adopted per-se. On the other hand, one might safely say "we are adopting the Scrum process framework" or "we are adopting Agile practices".

Transformation implies a change from one way of being to another way of being. This is something BIG. Like a caterpillar changing to a butterfly. Or creating an environment where people have joy at work.

"We are transforming to Agile." is an accurate way to describe what is undertaken in environments where the change represents a fundamental shift in behaviours and values.

The word *transition* means "movement, passage, or change from one position, state, stage, subject, concept, etc., to another". Transition could be used to describe either adoption or transformation. Since it is ambiguous, it is best to avoid this term altogether.

A Framework for Understanding Adoption and Transformation

Consider the following framework to allow us to analyze and effectively plan change efforts. In it there are three main categories as illustrated in the diagram below:

1. Adoption of Agile Practices in a Mismatched Culture (on left)

2. Adoption and Transformation in a Supportive Culture (middle)

3. Agile Transformation (on right)

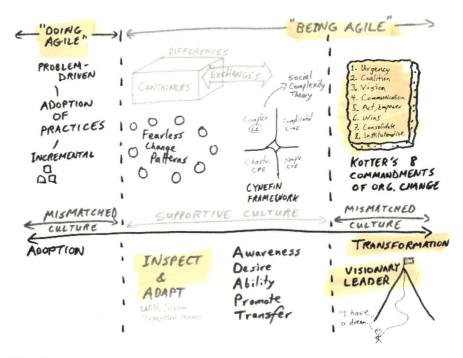

The diagram shows a range of approaches and in what context they are most useful. It is not intended for this view to be exhaustive, but rather illustrative of how well an approach is geared for adoption versus transformation. It provides a framework for thinking about the different approaches and goals in change work so that a change agent can select the right approach for a given context.

Adoption of Agile Practices in Mismatched Culture

The purpose of this section is to explain approaches to adopt Agile, Kanban or Software Craftsmanship practices in a company culture that is mismatched to the cultural system of the approach at hand. For example, this could be Agile practices (Collaboration/Cultivation culture) in a Control culture or Craftsmanship practices (Competence culture) in a Collaboration culture. The jigsaw puzzle illustration is used to show a piece-wise extension of the existing organizational structure. Before embarking on this, it is useful to consider a variety of perspectives around the merits of this type of approach.

The guidance provided by Schneider is to identify *practices* that support the dominant culture of the company or group rather than to try and change it. He calls this *making your culture work.*

Using Agile as an example, we would view it like a menu of practices rather than a value system. We might choose iterations or timeboxes to provide more structure and control to project delivery. Or introduce velocity to add empirical control to improve delivery predictability.

Many proponents of Agile find the notion of reducing it to a set of practices to be missing the whole point. One could make the argument that Agile is a way of helping organizations become more successful, not a set of practices to be selected piecemeal. From a culture perspective, Agile is about getting away from Control culture, not for finding ways to support it!

Another view to consider is that of *supplication* [Sirajuddin]. I think of supplication as a way of engaging with a person or system with a deep respect and appreciation. For example, rather than thinking "Wow, this department is really messed up", one might instead think "The system is performing as well as it can right now. People are able to accomplish things despite many obstacles." From a stance of supplication, we can see that perhaps an organization is not capable of accepting or even wanting an Agile mindset and instead support it at its current stage of learning and growth (i.e. culture).

Avoid Agile Manifesto and Scrum   HMMM?

Almost as important as what to do is what not to do. A key example is to avoid anything that might suggest or encourage a change in mindset or culture. Why? In my experience, it is confusing, disorienting, and hazardous to discuss a mindset shift when adopting practices. For example, focus on deep collaboration doesn't play well when a software group is split across the globe.

As discussed earlier, the Agile Manifesto is a statement of values that intends to form a specific culture. So it is a good idea to avoid mentioning them or even holding them as a goal when adopting Agile. At best, they are irrelevant and at worst they will cause accidental changes in staff behavior that creates friction in the environment. It is, however, worthwhile talking with the management team about culture together with Agile values and principles so that they may make an informed decision about adoption vs. transformation.

Scrum as a Disruptive Transformative Technology

Scrum is a very powerful transformative technology. Scrum is designed to disrupt existing power and control structures by creating new roles (Product Owner, Scrum Master, the Team). It also posits self-organizing teams as the fundamental building block of organizations. As such, it should be avoided if at all possible when adopting Agile practices in a mismatched culture. The reason for this is that it will by its very nature force culture transformation rather than allow adoption of practices. It is fine to use practices from Scrum however it is advisable to use vanilla Agile terms (e.g. Iteration, not Sprint) as discussed here [Sahota - "StealthScrum"].

Lean differentiates between *kaizen* (continuous improvement) and *kaikaku* (radical overhaul). Kanban advocates kaizen while Scrum is a form of kaikaku [Sahota – "Kanban is a Gateway Drug"]. In the event that there are strong environmental drivers for radical changes, then Scrum is a great choice for transformation. However, adoption with a mismatched culture is not such a situation.

Agile Adoption Patterns

Another great resource for adopting Agile practices is "Agile Adoption Patterns: A Roadmap to Organizational Success" [Elssamadisy]. He advocates pain-driven adoption of practices based on business smells (e.g. Features are not used) and process smells (e.g Lack of Visibility). Each smell or problem type is mapped to a set of Agile practices that address that problem. Here is an example:

> Problem: Hardening phase is needed at the end of the release cycle.

> Applicable Practices: Automated developer tests, continuous integration, functional tests, done state, and release often.

The approach outlined here is entirely about Agile practices – perfect for adopting Agile in a mismatched culture.

Becoming Agile in an Imperfect World

The book "Becoming Agile in an Imperfect World" provides a lot of practical advice on adopting Agile [Smith & Sidky]. The authors begin with the premise that many companies are not ready for Agile along a variety of dimensions: Tools, Culture, Project Management, Software Process and Physical Environment. They advocate becoming as Agile as possible given the current environmental limitations and most important needs. Although they recognize that Agile represents a shift in thinking, they support an incremental practices-oriented adoption that is suitable for adopting Agile practices in a mismatched culture.

Case Study: Large Financial

Consider the following situation: out-of-control "Agile" project at a large financial services company. People working on the project are in several locations in North America, have several off-shore sites, cross-matrix reporting and a Control/Competence culture. Agile was seen as a way to "get things done" and there was no organizational support for shifting to an Agile mindset or empowering people.

The result of the culture survey is as shown below. It is worth noting that during a group discussion of culture, it became clear that Control culture was dominant with Competence a secondary.

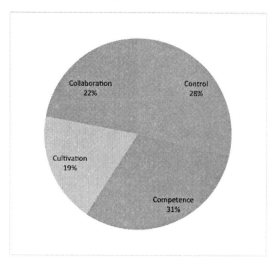

In the past (without my understanding of culture), I would for sure have looked for ways to help the client become more Agile or pushed for organizational change. The results would likely have been disastrous. A similar scenario arose at a telco where I was coaching and I helped contribute to Agile failure by advocating the Agile mindset. There have been other instances as well.

To succeed, I applied context and pain-driven adoption of various practices – some of them were Agile, some were not. One problem was that no one knew what scope could be delivered by the release date. The Agile practices applied were: face to face communication via a 3 day collocated workshop to "tuneup" the project. Another was Scrum-style burndown of the 6 week release backlog. Note: with 6 weeks to go, Iterations were dropped as they were not being followed anyway and did not seem to be delivering the usual benefits. An example of a non-Agile practice was use the Gallup employee engagement survey to measure business unit performance [Buckingham & Coffman]

After an intensive strategic planning process using the A3 Technique [Sahota – "A3 Technique"] it became clear that organizational impediments such as site/geographic strategy and matrix reporting would make it very difficult to shift the culture from Control and Competence in any meaningful way or even to build small collocated teams that could support this process. The environment is so constrained that anything beyond Agile practice adoption is not feasible at this time.

Adoption and Transformation in a Supportive Culture

In this section we consider what it means to adopt Agile or transform to Agile in a supportive culture where dominant cultures are Collaboration and Cultivation or perhaps Competence for an XP-oriented adoption. Although the ideas and approaches are suitable for Kanban or Software Craftsmanship, Agile will be used to illustrate the key ideas of this section.

As discussed earlier, the Schneider model provides a coarse lens through which to view organizational culture. The naïve view would be to confirm cultural alignment of an organization and proceed to simply proceed to adopt Agile practices under the assumption that the Agile mindset is fully supported by the culture. Unfortunately, the situation is somewhat more complex than this. So, the Schneider model helps us understand we are in this scenario, but provides no further guidance.

In Organizational Culture and Leadership, Schein argues, "we must avoid the superficial models of culture and build on the deeper, more complex anthropological models." [Schein, p.14]. He outlines many different dimensions to culture such as: customs, traditions, group norms, espoused values, formal philosophy, rules of the game, root metaphors, etc.

Further, the culture of a group is the aggregate of each individual's outlook. So it will generally be the case that some individuals do not conform to the overall culture. Agile tends to make these types of discrepancies very visible and promote certain types of behaviour such as collaboration and visibility.

Taken together it is clear that even if working with Agile in a supportive culture, it may well be the case that some level of individual and group transformation is required. The purpose of this section is to explore such approaches and to highlight their benefits and challenges.

Lead with Agile Manifesto and Scrum

When working with a culture that is already aligned with Agile values, then it is valuable to use the Agile Manifesto's values and principles as the cornerstone of the change initiative. When people are oriented to the purpose of the change initiative that Agile is supporting (the WHY), they are better able to avoid getting distracted by process details (the WHAT and the HOW).

32

Scrum plays well in this situation since it is by design a disruptive transformational technology. As discussed earlier it represents a radical overhaul of the organizational structure. In particular, its focus on autonomous self-organizing teams is particularly powerful for shifting to an Agile mindset.

Fearless Change

Fearless Change: Patterns for Introducing New Ideas provides lots of great techniques and tips for adopting new ideas within an organization [Manns & Rising]. The image below by Mihai Iancu shows a variety of different patterns that can be applied to support the adoption of a new technology or idea. I have used these patterns and they are very helpful – especially when one is feeling stuck and looking for some ideas to get going. I have included them on the adoption end of the scale because they are designed to introduce new ideas, not to transform organizational culture.

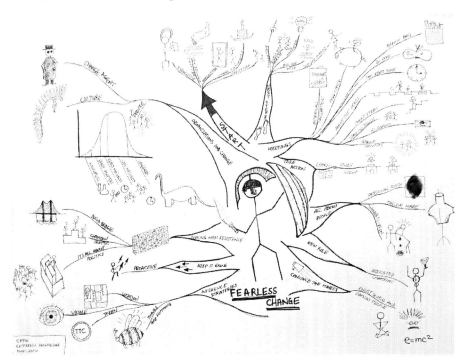

For a large image, please see [Iancu]

Deb Hartmann has created a game, Fearless Journey, to help people learn and apply these patterns [Hartmann].

When to use Fearless Change Patterns

Fearless change is a good toolkit to support a change initiative. As such it is suitable to support Agile adoption or to supplement another approach.

Inspect and Adapt with Enterprise Transition Team

The Enterprise and Scrum outlines how to "transition" (not transform) an organization to Scrum [Schwaber]. Note that the approach does not make explicit whether this is adoption or transformation. The key steps are as follows: *Agile transformation working Group*

1. ✓ Create an Enterprise Transition Team – a Scrum team responsible for the transition of the organization to Scrum.

2. ✓ Create an enterprise backlog of transition items.
   Using Leffingwell Framework to execute Transformation
3. ✓ Transition team executes Scrum; Inspect and adapt to success.
   Done this

Although it is acknowledged that Scrum requires a new Enterprise Culture and huge effort to execute – the book is missing specifics as to how to make this happen. One might even make a cynical remark that all we need to do is "inspect and adapt" our way to success. To my knowledge, this is the *most commonly applied pattern* within the community. See also A CIO's Playbook for Adopting the Scrum Method of Achieving Software Agility [Schwaber, Leffingwell and Smits].

It is worth noting the usage of the word *transition* that, as noted earlier, is ambiguous with respect to adoption and transformation. *The vagueness of the word "transition" is a great source of confusion* in the Agile coaching community around this topic.

When to use Inspect and Adapt

Inspect and adapt with an enterprise transition team is a reasonable approach for adopting Agile in very straightforward situations. In the event that change effort is more demanding, then a more powerful, transformational approach should be considered.

ADAPT

ADAPT is Mike Cohn's model for adoption of Scrum:

1. **Awareness** that the current process is not delivering acceptable results.

2. **Desire** to adopt Scrum as a way to address current problems.

3. **Ability** to succeed with Scrum.

4. **Promotion** of Scrum through sharing experiences so that we remember and others can see our successes.

5. **Transfer** of the implications of using Scrum throughout the company.

See Mike Cohn's book or presentation for further details [Cohn – "Succeeding with Agile" - Chapter 2] [Cohn – "Adapting to Agile Keynote"].

It is interesting to note that the model is moving in the direction of transformation, but not entirely there. See for example, how this compares with a thorough model for transformation such as the Kotter model where "desire" is replaced by "a sense of urgency". The latter being a much more demanding criteria. For example, I may be aware and desire to lose weight, but it might be too much effort so that I do not have a sense of urgency about it. An idea that is in line with transformation is the acknowledgement that transformation is about individuals: "All individuals will need to move through the Awareness, Desire, and Ability stage." On the other hand the basic mechanisms for executing this change are very much in line with the above "Inspect and Adapt with Enterprise Transition Team".

ADAPT can be seen as a complementary to the Inspect and Adapt model that provides some guidance around how to achieve organizational alignment around the move to Agile. It is for this reason that it is placed further to the right (towards transformation) in the overview diagram.

When to use ADAPT

ADAPT is suitable for Agile Adoption scenarios where the change effort required to move to an Agile mindset is relatively low. Significant change efforts would benefit from a more explicit approach to transformation.

Containers, Differences and Exchanges

CDE (Containers, Differences, Exchanges) is a model for reasoning about how to effect change in a complex system.

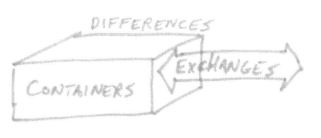

It is not an adoption model per-se but rather an approach for effecting change in organizations. CDE is a central component of a comprehensive approach that uses complexity thinking for organizational change [Olson and Eoyang].

CDE provides a way to understand the context of a team or group and highlights ways of effecting change. For example, a team is a very powerful container for organizing staff. So is the physical environment (E.g. team room). Exchanges are interaction points between containers such as email or financial transactions. Differences such as power or expertise are often key to understanding alignment and diversity. Esther Derby has a good post and presentation/video on Shifting Organizational Patterns [Derby]. CDE is also discussed elsewhere as an effective amplifier of an Agile change effort [Cohn -"Succeeding with Agile", p. 221-227].

When to use CDE

CDE helps one reason about how to influence a system. Consider using CDE as a supporting tool or complexity thinking for an emergent approach to change.

Cynefin Framework

Cynefin is a sense-making framework that recognizes the causal differences that exist between system types and proposes new approaches to decision-making in complex social environments. Some argue that the Cynefin model can be used to aid Agile adoption. Others use it as an analysis model to create a shared understanding of the type of environment so that the most appropriate approach can be selected.

The Cynefin model describes five different domains: Simple, Complicated, Complex, Chaotic and Disorder (the black bit in the middle). The first four are listed in order of decreasing causality whereas disorder is a human space where we simply do not know what type of system we are in. In a simple

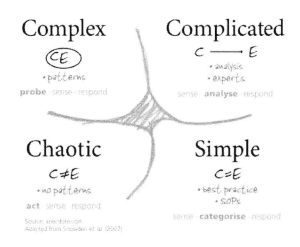

domain cause and effect are directly connected, whereas in a Chaotic domain there are no patterns and the relationship between cause and effect are unclear. We will consider Complicated and Complex domains further as they are more relevant when working with organizations.

For example, in complex environments, causes are understandable retrospectively (i.e. with hindsight) so that an adaptive approach to change is appropriate.

The implications for Agile adoption/transformation is clear – it is suggested that many organizational environments are complex and the transformation approach needs to reflect this reality or suffer failure. In a complex environment, we will not know what actions will lead to the desired result. Instead, we need to probe the environment, sense the result of our action and then select an appropriate response. This conceptual model implies that the environment can provide much less clarity in comparison to an Enterprise transition backlog.

Some aspects of organizational contexts are merely complicated and amenable to analysis. Systems Thinking is an example of a practice that requires a complicated environment to function [Senge]. A particularly useful analysis tool is cause-effect diagrams [Kniberg]. For example, as part of an A3 process, I have used cause-effect diagrams to yield meaningful analysis and use them as a basis for generating countermeasures [Sahota – "A3 Technique"].

John McFadyen, a proponent of the Cynefin model, suggests that organizational contexts are normally reliant on humans and we make just about everything we touch complex. However, many would act as though it we "merely" complicated as they have a bias towards acting in this environment.

The Cynefin model provides us with a language for understanding and reasoning about the kind of environment we are working in. Here is a short video explanation of the Cynefin model [CognitiveEdge] as well as a presentation on why it matters. i.e. the case for Complex Adaptive Systems [Schenk]. If you are interested in using and experiencing the Cynefin Model, perhaps consider the game created for this purpose that uses Lego [Tomasini & Lewitz].

When to use the Cynefin Model

The Cynefin models helps one reason about the relationship between cause and effect in a system and select an appropriate cognitive approach for change work. Cynefin is not an adoption or transformation approach, but rather a tool to help change agents understand their stance and approach. As such, it is complementary to other approaches.

Case Study of Agile Adoption in a Supportive Culture

The purpose of this case study is to illustrate that cultural alignment with Collaboration and Cultivation cultures alone is not sufficient to determine compatibility and success. The organization is a world-wide group of independent practices. As can be seen from the culture survey results below the company would appear to be a reasonable candidate for Agile. These survey results were confirmed by a group workshop, but not the inference.

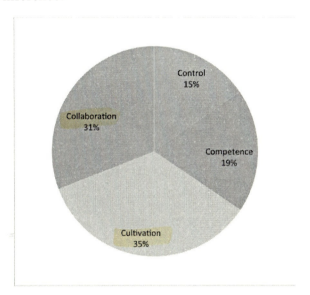

I was asked to "tune up" an existing Scrum team and adopt Agile practices with the another two small teams.

As part of an assessment/planning phase conducted prior to training and project launch, it became clear that a core part of the culture was unbridled individualism. A strong hero culture was in place and individual wishes for autonomous work were indulged by management. It became clear that perhaps Scrum might not be a good choice as it is far more disciplined than the environment could support at its stage of maturity. As a result of these and other concerns, the management team and I decided to use some of the time in the two day training to introduce Kanban in addition to Scrum. As well, we elected to make it a team-level decision as whether to adopt Scrum, Kanban or a mix of the two.

At the end of the training, all three teams selected Kanban over Scrum. Interestingly, the teams also adopted user stories, estimation and velocity to manage communication with stakeholders and to plan and track releases. A pairing workshop was also requested to support the goal of knowledge transfer. Only one team had a product owner. No team was ready to invest in a ScrumMaster or process coach.

Agile Transformation

The verb *transform* means [Merriam-Webster Dictionary]:

1. To change in composition or structure
2. To change the outward form or appearance of
3. To change in character or condition

The illustration of a caterpillar transforming into a butterfly is used to illustrate the deep changes that occur with transformation.

In the context of the Schneider culture model, a transformation would be a *shift from one core culture to another*.

In Agile terms, transformation is a *shift to an Agile Mindset* – which entails a shift in culture.

Is Agile Transformation Possible?

My conjecture is that *Agile alone is not sufficient to induce organizational transformation*. A related conjecture is that the Agile Adoption approaches discussed in the previous sections are insufficient for organizational transformation.

Kotter documents 10 large companies that have transformed their corporate culture [Kotter, Heskett]. So, it would appear that culture change is difficult, but possible.

Are there any documented cases of Agile transformation? I have heard people talk about Agile or Kanban inducing culture change. I am, at the time of this writing, not aware of any case studies to support either of these hypotheses.

Some people might point to the success of a company like SalesForce.com as an example of how they were able to change their culture. On the other hand, the article Six Common Mistakes that Salesforce didn't make, stated that "The leadership saw the transformation not so much as a wholly new approach, but rather a return to the firm's core values" [Denning]. So, this would then not be an example since the values in the leadership team did not change. It would seem that Agile in this case was used to address the drift in culture caused growth and introduction of middle management. I recall a similar story about getting back to the original culture with Yahoo, who also did an enterprise transition to Scrum.

Andrea Tomasini at Agile 42 and Hendrik Esser at Ericsson gave a case study at the 2012 Scrum Gathering in Atlanta where Scrum was used to guide a business unit of 2000 people to find its way after blowing up the hierarchy and matrix reporting. Scrum was instrumental in raising awareness and showcasing what was possible as well as executing the transformation to Agile. Management was pushed by changing market conditions and complaints, dissatisfaction and frustration from employees to consider change. Thus a key part of the transformation was when the management team shifted from operational concerns to spend six months working on reshaping the future of the company. It appears this kind of "cross the ocean and burn the boats" leadership is key to successful transformation. In this case Scrum acted as a catalyst for change but it was not the change process itself.

Radical Surgery

NUMMI was a joint venture where Toyota worked with GM to change the culture in one GM manufacturing plant [Shook – "NUMMI"]. Consider these excerpts around the result and the changes made:

"We took the quality of the plant from GM's very worst to GM's very best - not just bad to good, from worst to best - in only one year."

"I always point out, as I did above, that NUMMI's workforce was the same workforce that had been there before. That is true. What I sometimes don't have time to add is that, *true the workers were the same, but the managers ... all the managers were new*. They may have been from GM, from Toyota or hired from the outside, but they were new to NUMMI."

In this case, the culture shift was accomplished by replacing the entire management team. In most contexts this is not only infeasible but also undesirable. This is consistent with reports of middle management resistance being a key obstacle in transformation.

Transformation - One Person at a Time

What does it mean for an organization to transform?

Let us use the following definition of an organization: learning networks of people creating value [Appelo – "Stoos Network"]. An organization can only transform to the extent that the people in it undergo transformation. *Each person in the organization needs to progress through transformation at their own pace.* When an organization requires change at a faster rate than some individuals can deliver, this will result in staff changes with some leaving and some joining.

I think of Agile or any other system of organization culture as a virus that spreads and infects people. Through coaching teams with Agile, I can see when people "get it" and have made the jump to an Agile mindset. Resistance to the Agile virus (and change) differs between organizations and individuals.

Accidental Agile Transformation is Damaging Companies

Before embarking further, it is absolutely critical to make it clear that *the vast majority of organizations do not want transformation.* I have not yet worked with a company that understood what transformation was and wanted it. Over the past year when I have clarified with Agile practitioners what transformation is and represents only very small companies with visionary leadership were interested in transformation. It is generally the case that leaders and managers would like to have problems solved with as little effort and risk as possible. And transformation represents monumental effort and significant risk.

Consider the typical manager who would like to have Scrum adopted to improve her team's software process. She is probably thinking about Scrum as a process or process framework and not as a value system and mindset. She is unlikely to be aware that Scrum is a form of radical overhaul that requires significant management and staff support to avoid failure.

Even more alarming is that many Agile/Scrum practitioners and coaches are not yet aware of the disconnect between what is misunderstood about Scrum (it's a process) and what it actually entails (radical overhaul). A clear discussion of culture and the framework presented in this book would go a long way towards bridging this gap.

Many Change Agents Operate at an "Accidental" Skill Level

Based on my investigation into Agile failure, it is painfully clear that as a community we do not have enough clarity around what it means to adopt or transform to Agile and Scrum. Without a doubt many practitioners have a reasonable understanding of the mechanics (and to a much lesser extent) the mindsets of Agile and Scrum. What is sorely lacking is an understanding of the distinction between adoption and transformation. Consider the diagram below.

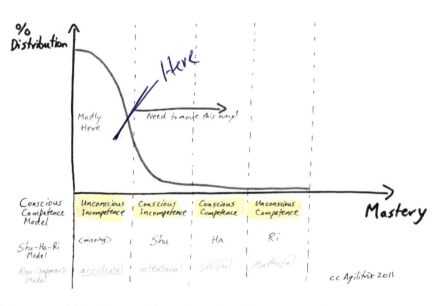

Let us consider the question of the skill level Agile change agents have in "helping organizations with Agile". It could be argued that many Agile change agents are just at the Shu level of Shu-Ha-Ri. However, there is a step before Shu – where someone does not know about or have interest in a particular skill – called *accidental* in Chapman's terminology and *unconscious incompetence* in the Conscious Competence Model.

I make the assertion that the vast majority of Agile change agents are at the accidental level. The key reasons are:

1. Failure to understand Agile as a system of culture and values

2. Failure to understand the disruptive power of Agile in general and Scrum in particular

3. Not understanding the difference between adoption and transformation

4. Often no explicit adoption or transformation framework

5. Weak or mis-alignment with management goals and objectives

The curved line depicts the current level of skill around Agile adoption/transformation. Please note that the line is notional as I only have qualitative information to support this claim. The bulk of the community is at the unconscious incompetence level with only a small number beyond this. Although there are some thought leaders sharing valuable insights, there is no coherent message that people agree on. We need to shift the curve to the right. My hope is that this book will help.

The days are over where we as a community can pretend that Agile is the greatest thing since sliced bread and just drop it into any company. The failure data simply does not support this notion. So let us now consider some models that actually do help with Agile transformation.

Kotter Model for Organizational Change

Truly transforming an organization requires consistent sustained energy over a long period of time. Kotter outlines the 8 steps that need to happen in sequence to establish real and lasting positive change.

TTOF Managing org change

These have been observed in a variety of companies over the last 20 years:

1. Establish a Sense of Urgency

2. Forming a powerful Guiding Coalition

KOTTER'S 8 COMMANDMENT. OF ORG. CHANGE

3. Creating a Vision

4. Communicating the Vision

5. Empowering Others to Act on the Vision

6. Planning for and Creating Short-Term Wins

7. Consolidating Improvements and Producing Still More Change

8. Institutionalizing New Approaches

The model is powerful, yet challenging to execute. For example, the criteria put forth for a *sense of urgency* is that *75% of management genuinely believe that the status quo is unacceptable.* In my experience, management may want and believe in Agile but fall well short of this criteria. When Agile practitioners I talk to fully comprehend this "minimum criteria" they are sad since they know that the companies they work with are nowhere close to this criteria. This effect helps explain the high levels of failure experienced today.

Consider a personal goal such as exercise. I may want to look after my body. I may know it's a good decision for my health. I may know that I will have more energy if I exercise. I may not want the negative consequences of excess weight and health risks. But that doesn't get me off the couch and out for a run. To succeed at improving my health, I need to acknowledge that the status quo is no longer working for me and commit to a sustained investment in my health.

Another key aspect of the model is that it is not possible to make real progress unless each step is completed in order. So, without a sense of urgency a change effort is doomed to failure. To learn more please see Kotter's book Leading Change [Kotter] Also, Olivier Lafontan has Card Decks for Implementing Kotter (very cool) if you are interested in using this model [Lafontan].

The implications of this model on Agile transformation is striking. It indicates that there must be an explicit and well-supported change effort in order to succeed. Lots of transition suggestions mention the need for "strong management support", but the call for urgency is a much clearer and compelling requirement.

At my CSM training in 2004, Ken Schwaber spoke of companies that were in really desperate situations (e.g. company survival) as good candidates for Scrum adoption since they had nothing to lose. It is clear in such circumstances that the first step – a sense of urgency – would be fully satisfied. Sadly, it is frequently the case these days that Scrum is "adopted" in organizations that lack this sense of urgency.

In my experience, many Agile change agents have done our industry a disservice by unwittingly *undertaking a transformation without full buy-in or understanding of the organizational consequences*. I believe that the overwhelming majority of Agile change agents are trying to do good in the world. For myself, I know there have been many occasions when I have wanted the client to fully move to Agile so that people are empowered and can produce great results. But this was my wish and dream, not the clients. The disconnect between good intentions and accidental transformation helps understand one root cause of the many failures we are seeing with Agile transformation.

Transformational Leadership

Edgar Schein talks about the key ways that leaders embed culture in the organization [Schein]. In his model, the primary embedding mechanisms are:

- What leaders pay attention to, measure, and control on a regular basis

- How leaders react to critical incidents and organizational crisis

- How leaders allocate resources

- Deliberate role modeling, teaching and coaching

- How leaders allocate rewards and status

- How leaders recruit, select, promote and excommunicate

It is possible for a leader at any level of a management hierarchy to introduce transformation within the span of their control. It is critical that transformation leaders make it clear that everyone in the system will need to change behaviours or leave for transformation to occur.

"Agile is about people, and as such they will tend to be the largest obstacles. We will need to have serious conversations at some point if we really want to go Agile." – Johnny Scarborough

> Case Study: At a large financial, on the first day of my engagement I had a frank conversation with the VP who hired me. I indicated that the team he was asking me to work with was a complex system and that he was part of that system. The consequence was that I would need to give him direct feedback on how his actions were or were not supporting the team. He agreed and I tested his openness the next day. He passed the test and we developed a great working relationship. As it turned out, he was ready to do what it took to support Agile, but in the end, the organization was not ready.

Leaders Go (Agile) First!

Jon Stahl reports an approach called Agile From the Top Down: Executives & Leadership Living Agile [Stahl]. I think of it as *how to incubate transformational leadership*. Leaders go first by doing the following:

- Live the values

- Lead by example

- Seek to truly understand their culture

- Be as transparent as the teams they lead

Before embarking on an Agile transformation, Jon shows a video showing a high-creativity environment to illustrate the Agile mindset [ABC Nightline]. Then he asks executives:

- Is this what you really want?

- Are you prepared to change your own behaviour to support this?

- Are you ready to go first?

Temenos Leadership Retreat

Temenos is the name given by Siraj Sirajuddin for an intensive retreat that assists people in understanding their deepest personal visions and how they want to influence the organizational, social and family containers around their lives. The heart of the workshop is around recognizing and appreciating ourselves and others as human beings. A central idea is that a leadership team needs to maintain it's own health and functioning as a primary objective. Like John Stahl's approach, this has the leaders "be the change they want to see." The main point of difference is that Temenos opens the way to have a shift in mindset in a very short time period.

Other Approaches to Organizational Change

It is not intended that this book completely cover all known approaches to organizational change that are used within the Agile community. That said, this section will serve as a very brief reading guide for those interested in exploring wider.

- Bob Marshall has created a model that describes an evolutionary path for organizations towards higher effectiveness called rightshifting that is characterized by the prevailing mindset [Marshall].

- Jurgen Appelo has a great slide deck and booklet on How to Change the World [Appelo]. In it he describes a supermodel composed of four models about 1) interacting with the system, 2) minding the people, 3) stimulating the adoption network, and 4) changing the environment. This includes: Plan-Do-Check-Act and Moore's Chasm model. It is interesting to note that he contrasts this with other change models such as Fearless Change and Switch [Heath].

Where to go next?

As a community, our understanding of Agile and its implications is an ongoing, evolving process. This book is a first step towards understanding the key cultural biases of Agile, Kanban and Software Craftsmanship. I have presented a guide for working with your existing culture as well as a framework for understanding key adoption and transformation approaches.

Checklist for Change Agents

Checklists are commonly used to avoid routine errors. Below is a checklist for Agile adoption and Transformation. This list is both for external and internal change agents. For an internal change agent, your client is the group you are helping adopt or transform to Agile.

1. I know what problem my client is asking me to solve

2. I understand the dominant and secondary cultures as well as the driving forces in the client environment

3. My client and I agree about the objectives and approach – just adopting practices or transforming the culture too

4. I am following an explicit adoption/transformation approach

5. My client has a good understanding of the implications of the proposed approach

6. My client and I agree about the scope of people included as well as impacted

7. My client is fully invested in making the required changes and has the required organizational support to execute successfully

8. The span of influence and control of my client is sufficient to make success possible

9. My client understands that when working with a complex system, the path taken is an emergent property that cannot be defined in advance.

References

ABC Nightline. *IDEO Shopping Cart*, 1999, *YouTube*, Web, <http://www.youtube.com/watch?feature=player_embedded&v=M66ZU2PCIcM>.

Anderson, David. *The Principles of the Kanban Method.* Web. 10 Dec. 2010. <http://agilemanagement.net/index.php/Blog/the_principles_of_the_kanban_method>.

Appelo, Jurgen. *How to Change the World* (slides). Web. 2011. <http://www.noop.nl/2011/09/how-to-change-the-world.html>

Appelo, Jurgen. *How to Change the World*. Lulu. eBook. 2012.

Appelo, Jurgen. *Stoos Network (part 3): Core Idea*. Web. 10 Jan. 2012. <http://www.noop.nl/2012/01/stoos-network-part-3-core-idea.html>.

Beck, Don Edward., and Christopher C. Cowan. *Spiral Dynamics: Mastering Values, Leadership and Change.* Oxford: Blackwell, 2006. Print.

Behrens, Pete. *The Culture of Agility*, Web. 2011, <http://trailridgeconsulting.com/culture-of-agility.html?view=slide>

Block, Peter. *Flawless Consulting: A Guide to Getting Your Expertise Used*. San Francisco: Jossey-Bass/Pfeiffer, 2000. Print

Buckingham, Marcus and Coffman, Curt. *First, Break All the Rules, What the World's Greatest Managers Do.* Simon & Schuster,, 1999. Print. <http://www.studergroup.com/newsletter/Vol1_Issue1/gallups12questions.htm>.

Burrows, Mike. *Kanban and the Twelve Principles of Agile Software*. Positive Incline. Web. 21 Jun. 2010. <http://positiveincline.com/?p=727>.

CognitiveEdge. "The Cynefin Framework." *YouTube*. YouTube, 11 July 2010. Web. 09 Mar. 2012. <http://www.youtube.com/watch?v=N7oz366X0-8>.

Cohn, Mike. *Succeeding with Agile: Software Development Using Scrum*. Upper Saddle River, NJ: Addison-Wesley, 2010. Print.

Cohn, Mike. *ADAPTing to Agile for Continued Success (Keynote)*. Web. 2010. <http://www.mountaingoatsoftware.com/presentations/137-adapting-to-agile-for-continued-success-keynote>.

Cottemeyer, Mike. *Untangling Adoption and Transformation*. Web. January. 2011. <http://www.leadingagile.com/2011/01/untangling-adoption-and-transformation>.

Denning, Steve. "Six Common Mistakes that Salesforce.com Didn't Make." Web. 18 April. 2011. <http://www.forbes.com/sites/stevedenning/2011/04/18/six-common-mistakes-that-salesforce-com-didnt-make/>.

Derby, Esther. "Shifting Organizational Patterns." Web. March. 2011. <http://www.estherderby.com/2011/03/shifting-organizational-patterns.html>.

Elssamadisy, Amr. *Agile Adoption Patterns: A Roadmap to Organizational Success*. Upper Saddle River, NJ: Addison-Wesley, 2009. Print.

Fowler, Martin. "SemanticDiffusion." Web. 14 Dec. 2006. <http://martinfowler.com/bliki/SemanticDiffusion.html>.

Gat, Israel. "How We Do Things Around Here in Order to Succeed." Web. Aug. 2010. <http://www.agilitrix.com/2010/08/how-we-do-things-around-here-in-order-to-succeed/>.

Hartmann, Bob. "Doing Agile Isn't The Same As Being Agile." *SlideShare*. Web. 12 Feb. 2010. <http://www.slideshare.net/lazygolfer/doing-agile-isnt-the-same-as-being-agile>.

Hartmann, Deborah. *Fearless Journey*. <http://fearlessjourney.info/>.

Heath, Chip and Heath, Dan. Switch: *How to Change Things When Change Is Hard*. 2010. Print.

Iancu, Mihai, Web. <http://agilitrix.com/wp-content/uploads/2010/03/Fearless-Change-Mindmap-by-Mihai-Iancu.jpg>.

Kotter, John and Heskett, James. *Corporate Culture and Performance.* 1992. Print.

Kotter, John P. *Leading Change*. Boston, MA: Harvard Business School, 1996. Print.

Kniberg, Henrik. *Cause-Effect Diagrams*. Web. 09 Mar. 2012. <http://blog.crisp.se/2009/09/29/henrikkniberg/1254176460000>.

Lafontan, Olivier. "Card Decks for Agile Transitions." Web. 08 June. 2010. <http://leanpizza.net/?page_id=63>.

"Manifesto for Agile Software Development." Web. 2001 <http://www.agilemanifesto.org/>.

"Manifesto for Software Craftsmanship." Web. 2009. <http://manifesto.softwarecraftsmanship.org/>.

Manns, Mary Lynn, and Linda Rising. *Fearless Change: Patterns for Introducing New Ideas*. Boston: Addison-Wesley, 2005. Print.

Marshall, Bob. *The Marshall Model of Organisational Evolution*. Web. 2010 <http://fallingblossoms.com/opinion/content?id=1006>

Martin, Robert. "Quintessence: the Fifth Element for the Agile Manifesto." Web. 14 Aug. 2008. <http://blog.objectmentor.com/articles/2008/08/14/quintessence-the-fifth-element-for-the-agile-manifesto>.

Martin, Robert. "The Land that Scrum Forgot." *Scrum Alliance*. Web. 14 Dec. 2010. <http://www.scrumalliance.org/articles/300-the-land-that-scrum-forgot>.

Mayer, Tobias. "The People's Scrum." Web. 06 Dec. 2009 <http://agileanarchy.wordpress.com/2009/12/06/the-peoples-scrum/>.

Mayer, Tobias. "Scrum: A New Way of Thinking." Web. 22 Mar. 2008. <http://agileanarchy.wordpress.com/scrum-a-new-way-of-thinking/>.

Merriam-Webster Dictionary, Web. 2012. <http://www.merriam-webster.com/dictionary/>.

Moore, Geoffrey A. *Crossing the Chasm: Marketing and Selling Disruptive Products to Mainstream Customers*. New York, NY: HarperBusiness Essentials, 2002. Print.

Olson, Edwin and Eoyang, Glenda. *Facilitating Organizational Change: Lessons from Complexity Science*. Jossey-Bass/Pfeiffer, 2001. Print.

Pelrine, Joseph "InfoQ." : *Dealing With the Organizational Challenges of Agile Adoption*. Web. 09 Mar. 2012. <http://www.infoq.com/presentations/Agile-Adoption-Joseph-Pelrine>.

Sahota, Michael. "A3 Technique". *Serious Problems? Use A3 Technique to Nail 'em!* <http://agilitrix.com/2010/07/use-a3-technique-to-solve-serious-problems/>

Sahota, Michael. *Kanban is a Gateway Drug.* Web 2010. <http://agilitrix.com/2010/06/kanban-is-a-gateway-drug>

Sahota, Michael. *Scrum or Kanban?* Yes! Web. May. 2012.
<http://agilitrix.com/2010/5/scrum-or-kanban-yes/>.

Sahota, Michael. *Vacation Stealth Scrum.* Web. May. 2005.
<http://www.slideshare.net/mobile/michael.sahota/vacation-stealth-scrum>.

Sahota, Michael, *Workshop Results on Culture.* Web. November 2011,
<http://agilitrix.com/2011/11/workshop-results-on-culture/>,

Scarborough, Johnny, 2011, Private communication

Schein, Edgar. *Organizational Culture and Leadership.* Print. 1996.

Schenk, Mark. *The Case for Complexity.* Web. 16 July. 2009.
<http://www.anecdote.com.au/archives/2009/07/the_case_for_co.html>.

Schneider, William E. *The Reengineering Alternative: A Plan for Making Your Current Culture Work.* Burr Ridge, IL: Irwin Professional Pub., 1994. Print.

Schneider, William. *Schneider Culture Survey.* SurveyMonkey. Web.
<http://www.surveymonkey.com/s/VVNT5FB>.

Schwaber, Ken. *The Enterprise and Scrum.* Redmond, WA: Microsoft, 2007. Print.

Schwaber, Leffingwell and Smits: *A CIO's Playbook for Adopting the Scrum Method of Achieving Software Agility.* Web. Published 2005.
<http://www.leffingwell.org/Document_Store/CIO_Playbook_For_Adopting_Scrum_080805.pdf>.

Scotland, Karl. *Thoughts on Kanban Thinking.* Web. Dec. 2011.
<http://availagility.co.uk/2011/12/03/thoughts-on-kanban-thinking/>.

Scotland, Karl. *Crystallising Kanban with Properties, Strategies and Techniques.* Web. Aug. 2011.

<http://availagility.co.uk/2011/08/03/crystallising-kanban-with-properties-strategies-and-techniques/>.

Senge, Peter M. *The Fifth Discipline: The Art and Practice of the Learning Organization*. New York: Doubleday/Currency, 2006. Print.

Shook, John. "How NUMMI Changed Its Culture." *Lean.org*. Web. 30 Sept. 2009. <http://www.lean.org/shook/displayobject.cfm?o=1166>.

Shook, John. *Managing to Learn: Using the A3 Management Process to solve problems, gain agreement, mentor and lead*. Web. July. 2010. Lean Enterprise Institute and Ocapt (in Canada).

Sirajuddin, Siraj. Private communication. 2010.

Smith, Greg, and Ahmed Sidky. *Becoming Agile: --in an Imperfect World*. Greenwich, CT: Manning, 2009. Print.

Spayd, Michael. *Agile & Culture: The Results*. Web. 06 July. 2010. <http://collectiveedgecoaching.com/2010/07/agile__culture>.

Stack Overflow, *Is Agile Development Dead?* Web. 19 Nov. 2008, <http://stackoverflow.com/questions/301993/is-agile-development-dead>.

Stahl, Jon. *Agile From the Top Down: Executives & Leadership Living Agile*. SlideShare. Web. 09 Aug. 2011. <http://www.slideshare.net/LeanDog/agile-from-the-top-down>.

Thomas, Dave, "Dave Thomas Unplugged" Web. Aug. 2010. <http://agilitrix.com/2010/08/agile-2010-keynote-by-dave-thomas>.

Tomasini, Andrea and Lewitz, Olaf. "Cynefin Lego Game." Web. 25 Dec. 2011. <http://www.agile42.com/blog/2011/12/25/cynefin-leg-game/>.

VersionOne, *State of Agile Development Survey Results.* Web. 09 Mar. 2012. <http://www.versionone.com/state_of_agile_development_sur vey/11/>.

Wikimedia Foundation. "Hype Cycle." *Wikipedia.* 08 March. 2012. Web. <http://en.wikipedia.org/wiki/Hype_cycle>.

About the Author

"As the principal consultant of Agilitrix, my mission is to make a difference in the lives of the people and the companies I work with. Although I am a thought leader, use innovative approaches, and a wide set of tools, my main strength is the energy and passion I bring as a change artist to help my clients realize their goals. Sure the goal is to get better, but we can do that and put a smile on everyone's face."

As Agile/Lean Coach, Consultant and Trainer in Toronto, I work with businesses to accelerate delivery of value.

With software teams, this may include introducing modern software delivery frameworks such as Scrum or Kanban. I help Product Managers collaborate with stakeholders and customers to get great results through Innovation Games®.

Operational groups may benefit more from the application of Lean practices such as Value Stream Mapping, Kaizen and Kanban to improve efficiency.

My passion right now is around using play to unleash creativity and achieve breakthrough results. In addition to a variety of games and simulations, I am also trained in StrategicPlay® with Lego® SERIOUS PLAY® for solving wicked problems. I also facilitate Open Space workshops to bring large groups together on tough problems.

Appendix I: Alternate Views and Opinions

This section provides a voice for people who hold alternate views to those presented in this book.

It serves to remind us as Henrik pointed out in the foreword that no one has all the answers and that we need to think for ourselves.

Culture as Context for Agile Adoption and Transformation
by Olaf Lewitz

Context is more than culture

I fully agree that to "survive an agile transformation" we need to pay more attention to culture. Yet to focus on culture as the singe most important challenge an agile transformation faces is risky. Culture is but one aspect of the context, the system we work with, others being prevailing mindset (ad-hoc, analytical, synergistic, chaordic), business situation, technical "situation" (technical debt, technical excellence...), organisational situation (silos, dislocation, ...). Which one of these (the list is not complete) is the most important challenge to your agile transformation depends on your context, and your goals.

Which leads to my personal assumption for the #1 challenge: wrong goals. Many organisations attempting an agile transition/adoption do it for the wrong reasons (costs, doing the wrong things righter), underestimate the effects on people when you emancipate them, and/or fully fail to understand why and how Agile works in the first place.

Agile is not a good/best practice

Agile is a way to find an emergent solution in a complex domain. It is an evolutionary approach to innovation and growth, respecting the people who create value. Done right, it inspires and facilitates a transformation of mindset and culture of knowledge work organisations. Catalyst is the adoption of certain (good) practices like a daily standup and a visual board. These adoptions change how people collaborate and inspire them to re-think their workplace. New practices emerge if this improvement process continues. They will never be similar in two different organisations. Agile can not be standardised.

Indicators for choosing the method

There are a lot of aspects of a system that might influence your choice for an agile "flavour" (Scrum, Kanban, XP, ...) as a starting point. The business model for the service or product developed is the main factor I take into consideration, yet there are multiple others.

You should be interested in the culture, sense the contrasting influences in it (I almost always see a mix of the four Schneider types) and get a feeling for possible dissonances. As Agile challenges the status quo, you should know what you're challenging. Challenging a culture requires respecting it, not adapting to it.

Some examples to illustrate my point: a competence culture (google comes to mind) might just need something like Scrum to inspire people to collaborate. A "control" culture might need a disruptive challenge to actually change... And in a culture where collaboration is already a strength, Kanban might be a useful tool to visualise and improve flow (and to identify bottlenecks caused by lacks in competence...)

Organisations are multiple-faceted beings, we need to pay attention to more aspects than "just" the prevailing or apparent culture.

Your Kanban is not my Kanban

Karl Scotland writes:

Here I This has got me thinking about how I would place the various elements of Kanban Thinking (http://availagility.co.uk/2011/12/03/thoughts-on-kanban-thinking/).

Systems Thinking - probably covers the whole framework :)

Flow - Control (being /under/ control [stable] rather than /having/ control)
Value - Cultivation, but probably close to competence
Capability - Competence, but probable close to cultivation

Study - Collaboration (collectively understanding the current state)
Share - Collaboration (visualisation is a form of sharing knowledge)
Limit - Control (limits are a means of stabilising a system)
Sense - Competence (how good are we now)
Learn - Cultivate (how can we get better)

Which interestingly gives two in each quadrant :)

Kanban is more than just Control Culture

Alexei Zheglov writes:

I have a number of disagreements with the chapter "Kanban Culture is Aligned with Control." I would draw the Kanban culture diagram (p. 18) very differently. I'd like to offer these differences as part of feedback.

I believe "visualize the workflow" belongs in the Collaboration quadrant. Visual boards are essential collaboration tools. They are the opposite of some project manager's "visualizing" things in MS Project. Kanban visualizes the flow of work items along the value streams, which is different from other visualizations common to control-type organizations, such as org charts and KPI dashboards. (Michael Sahota: I partly agree. In the diagram, it is on the border, close to collaboration quadrant)

Limit WIP is what science tells us to do, so I associate it with the Competence quadrant. "Peter, if you could do X by the end of the day, that would be great" happens a lot in the Control culture. It is push and doesn't respect WIP limits. Pulling and limiting WIP is the opposite. By science I mean queueing theory (Little's Law) and psychology (as there are psychological effects of limited WIP). (Michael Sahota: Great observation! There is a tension between process aspects and efficiency. I will update diagram to reflect a balance between these.)

In "make process policies explicit", "process" and "policies" are attributes of Control, but "explicit" suggests visualization and ownership by the team. I'd place it on the borderline.

"Manage flow": David Anderson also refers to it in the same blog post (http://agilemanagement.net/index.php/Blog/the_principles_of_the_kan ban_method/) as "measure flow." This principle is also referred to as "measure and manage flow." "Measure" is an important word here, because it means measuring something in a way similar to how measurements are made in a scientific experiment. And then we manage the flow based what we measured. I'd place this principle on the borderline or maybe entirely in the Competence quadrant. (Michael Sahota: Another good observation. I will update diagram to reflect this.)

Overall, my version of the Kanban culture diagram is an L-shaped blob, stretching from Collaboration to Control and then into the Competence quadrant - rather than a circle centered in Control. It doesn't change your overall conclusion, however - Kanban as a tool complementary to the "traditional" Agile methods and craftsmanship.

Kanban is about Transformation, too!

Jeff Anderson writes:

My take is that Kanban has a better chance of *appealing to control cultures*, than agile does. But that is a comment about marketing, not about what the method requires to function, or where it works best.

My main concern is that slicing up major agile methods by cultural quadrant may require too much generalization. Organizations I work with seem to defy this primary slotting of a quadrant, and I find that Kanban, Agile, etc have to many overlapping pieces to neatly match a quadrant. I agree that we can get in over our head when it comes to applying agile without regard to context, and I also get the impression that many out there are not even aware of what they need to learn. That took bravery on your part to say, well done.

My final counter assertion is that I do believe Agile transformation is very possible. But the best chance is *through incremental agile adoption.*

My take is that culture is a by-product of the practice and way people work. The way they work with each other, their clients, and their bosses. So if you can change the work, then eventually culture will follow, and transformation can happen, it is just SLOW.

I tend to agree that quick radical transformation is reserved for companies about to go bankrupt, this makes it not a very interesting topic for me.

Scrum vs. Kanban

Jon Stahl writes:

We use Kanban for teams that are attempting to practice Scrum but, because they are structured wrong, they cannot succeed as a self organizing team.

Kanban practice allows us to:

- expose policies that are wasteful and need to be challenged

- use limits & data to validate that people may be in the wrong roles to support consistent flow

- ensure that the whole team is accountable for the whole process, not just their piece

Kanban allows us to start applying systems thinking as a whole team so that we can identify and remove waste. Seeing the whole system helps reduce the need for protective barriers and makes conversations with other teams easier. So, for me, Kanban isn't so much about command & control as much as it is understanding flow AS A TEAM. Once they understand the value of tokens and how the system works, they can adaptively move to a better process.